ENDANGERED SPECIES:
Flora & Fauna in Peril

WILDLING ART MUSEUM

LOS OLIVOS, CALIFORNIA

2008

ENDANGERED SPECIES:
Flora & Fauna in Peril

Art Competition & Exhibition

Sponsored by the Wildling Art Museum

Funded in part by the Dancing Star Foundation

JUNE 22 – SEPTEMBER 14, 2008
WILDLING ART MUSEUM, LOS OLIVOS, CA

NOVEMBER 1, 2008 – FEBRUARY 28, 2009
U.S. DEPARTMENT OF THE INTERIOR MUSEUM, WASHINGTON, D.C.

MAY 9 – JULY 12, 2009
THE WILDLIFE EXPERIENCE, PARKER, CO

WILDLING ART MUSEUM *America's Wilderness in Art*

2329 Jonata Street • PO Box 907 • Los Olivos, CA 93441

www.wildlingmuseum.org

Consulting Curator/Tour Director: David J. Wagner, Ph.D.

Exhibition and Catalogue Coordinator/Editor: Cynthia Anderson

Catalogue Design and Production: Kimberly Kavish Design

Reproduction Photography: William B. Dewey

Digital Image Assistance: Bill Dahl and Tom Buhl

Assistant to the Catalogue Coordinator: Nicole Flores

*Special thanks to Valerie Fellows, Public Affairs Specialist,
U.S. Department of Fish & Wildlife, for her assistance
with species names and identification.*

Printed in the USA
Haagen Printing, Santa Barbara, California

ISBN: 978-0-615-20705-6

DONORS

DANCING STAR FOUNDATION:

A very special thank you to the Dancing Star Foundation, who led the way by providing a challenge grant to help make the Endangered Species competition, exhibition, and catalogue possible; and who supplemented that amount with an additional grant when the challenge was exceeded.

DONORS FOR PRIZE AWARDS:

First Prize: Nancy and Joseph Byrne

Second Prize: Louise B. Clarke and John Carbon; Heloise and Alexander Power

Third Prize: Susan Bower

BUSINESS SPONSOR:

Haagen Printing

THE FOLLOWING DONORS GAVE GENEROUSLY TO MATCH THE DANCING STAR FOUNDATION'S CHALLENGE GRANT:

Isabel and Victor Bartolome
Joan and Merle Blasjo
William S. Burtress
Rick and Carol Bury
Dennis L. Cabral
Sarah Chamberlin and
    Benjamin Bottoms
Nancy Chase
Carnzu Clark
Louise B. Clarke and John Carbon
Martha Clyde
Roger and Joan Craton
Anne G. Cushing in memory
    of John E. Cushing
Oswald Da Ros
Katie Dabney
William and Carol Davidson
Janet W. Davis
Margaret Jo Dawes and
    Della Jean Elden
Nan Deal
Bernard and Marcie Drury
Jack and Debbie Duckworth
Mrs. Ian N. Dundas
Judith Etchelecu and
    P. Edward Prutzman
Gordon and Constance Fish
Diane and Richard Fly
Dan and Debbie Gerber
Frank and Judith Ghezzi
Myron Gretler
Oscar and Elizabeth Guidali
Sarah Hall

Ed and Ann Hammond
John and Katherine Hancock
John and Susan Hanna
Doug and Sue Herthel
Eric and Elena Hochberg
Florence Hundley
Elsie Hunt
Mary and John Hunt
Bobbi Hunter
Elizabeth Hvolbøll
Eric P. Hvolbøll
Krystyna Jackson
Robert and Carol Jackson
Eleanor Jacobs
Frank and Barbara Jameson
Karin E. Jamison, M.D.
Brian and Terry Jarchow
Joe and Lisa Johnston
Carol Kenyon, South Coast Fine
    Arts Conservation Center
Penny and Joe Knowles
Edie and Tom Kuhr
Barbara and Henry Larsen
Frederick and Linda Lee
Bob and Linda Leite
Sharron and Ferdinand Luft
Charlie and Lisa Markham
Cynthia Martin
Jim and Roxanne Mattinson
Pat and Riley McClelland
Mike and Sigi McCormack
Suzanne and Duncan Mellichamp
Marlene and Warren Miller

Alfred Moir
Arthur and Barbara Najera
Gary and Anna Nett
Joanna Bard Newton
Barbara V. O'Grady and
    John Prebish
Julie and Will Obering
Edith H. Overly
Art Polan
Paul and Mary Anne Prince
Eugene H. Reish
Gilbert and Ines Roberts
Alexander and Dale Rossi
Allen and Diana Russell
Peter Schuyler and Lisa Stratton
Ruth B. Scollin
Mike and Tresha Sell,
    Rio Vista Chevrolet
Tom and Dona Senning
Carol M. Smith
Lillian Smith
Virginia Souza
Patricia B. Sprowls
Evelyn E. Sullivan
Mathew Tekulsky
Herbert and Karen Tews
Phillip I. and Barbara Tullis
Jo Beth Van Gelderen
Deanne G. Violich
Suzanne L. Weakley
Harold Williams and
    Nancy Englander

CONTENTS

FOREWORD

By Elizabeth P. Knowles

HOLLY CLINE

THE WORD "WILDLING" means a "wild or uncultivated plant" or "wild animal"—a suitable name for the Wildling Art Museum, dedicated to presenting the art of America's wilderness. Since the Museum opened in Los Olivos, California, in 2000, we have organized over thirty exhibitions featuring artists like Ansel Adams and Bob Kuhn, as well as group shows exploring broader themes.

From the Museum's inception, the leadership dreamed of organizing an important international juried art competition. To this end, we enlisted the assistance of David J. Wagner, Ph.D., a scholar of American wildlife art experienced in organizing competitions and traveling exhibitions. The topic of endangered species seemed both timely and interesting to a broad spectrum of artists.

The call for entries was announced in June 2006. Our competition rules specified that eligible species must appear on the U.S. Fish & Wildlife Service's (USFWS) list of threatened and endangered species in North America. We soon discovered that this list is fluid, with species continually added or deleted depending upon environmental and political factors. For example, the bald eagle was de-listed in the lower 48 states in July 2007, but we considered those entries because the species was still listed when our competition was announced. (Of special note, in March 2008 the bald eagle was re-listed in the Sonoran

Desert region of central Arizona.) Unfortunately, though the listing of the polar bear is certainly warranted, we had to exclude that species since the USFWS had not taken action by our deadline.

It can be difficult to locate threatened or endangered species and "capture" them artistically without harming them. Advanced lenses and shutter speeds aid photographers in this process, and many painters and sculptors utilize photographs for their references. Botanical artists, unable to pull up endangered species as did illustrators of yore, must rely on historic specimens to depict the roots. I admire the artists who struggled with these issues to submit such visually stunning entries. Thanks to the discernment of our distinguished jury, the Wildling Art Museum is proud to present an exhibition that will inform and delight—varied not only in the flora and fauna represented, but also in style and media.

I am especially grateful to Dr. Michael Tobias and Jane Gray Morrison of the Dancing Star Foundation for their intellectual and financial contributions to this project, to David J. Wagner for his expert guidance, to Cynthia Anderson for so brilliantly managing the details, and to Kimberly Kavish for the catalogue design. I particularly thank our donors who provided substantial cash awards for the winning entries and who made this exhibition and catalogue possible.

Elizabeth P. Knowles
Executive Director
Wildling Art Museum

INTRODUCTION

By David J. Wagner, Ph.D.

MARQUAND BOOKS

David J. Wagner, Ph.D., *is president of a limited liability corporation that produces traveling exhibitions and provides curatorial, educational, and museum management services nationwide. He and his company have produced exhibitions and tours such as* Art and the Animal *for the Society of Animal Artists and* Blossom ~ Art of Flowers *for the Susan K. Black Foundation. He has also organized landmark conferences, including* Value in American Wildlife Art *at the Chautauqua Institute (1992) and* World Wildlife Art *at the Björklunden campus of Lawrence University (2000). His most recent publication is* American Wildlife Art *(Marquand Books, 2008, www.american-wildlife-art.com).*

THE JURIED EXHIBITION *Endangered Species: Flora & Fauna in Peril* was conceived to recognize, promote, and reward excellence in art, as well as heighten public awareness about threatened and endangered species in North America.

The U.S. Endangered Species Act of 1973—which evolved out of the Endangered Species Preservation Act of 1966 and the Endangered Species Conservation Act of 1969—remains the most significant legislation inspired by the environmental movement. The act defines categories of threatened and endangered species and requires all Federal agencies to undertake programs for their conservation.

As I explain in my book *American Wildlife Art,* species designated as threatened or endangered and the habitats they populate have been portrayed by many noteworthy twentieth-century wildlife artists. Ray Harm (b. 1926), for example, created *Bald Eagle* for publication as his first limited edition print in 1963, prefiguring its designation as an endangered species. In 1969, he and other artists represented by his publishing company donated signed, limited edition prints to the National Audubon Society to raise money for the preservation of Corkscrew Swamp, a wildlife sanctuary near Naples, Florida.

Twenty years later, Canadian painter Robert Bateman (b. 1930) pushed wildlife art further into the arena of environmental activism with works such as *Carmanah Contrasts*, a controversial painting that contrasted old-growth and clear-cut forest imagery of Vancouver Island's Carmanah Forest; and *Mossy Branches—Spotted Owl,* a portrait of a seemingly benign bird in its native habitat, but in fact a powerful symbol of a highly charged logging issue. A poster child for environmentalism, the northern spotted owl was officially listed as a threatened species in 1990. Bateman continued his environmental foray with other brave and powerful paintings, notably *Self-portrait with Big Machine and Ancient Sitka* and *Driftnet (Pacific White-sided Dolphin & Lysan Albatross),* a painting that exposes the grim realities of commercial fishing.

On March 24, 1989, one of the worst manmade ecological disasters of all time occurred when the *Valdez,* an oil tanker owned by Exxon Corporation, ran aground and leaked an estimated eleven million gallons of crude oil into Prince William Sound. The tragedy moved sculptor Kent Ullberg (b. 1945) to create *Requiem for Prince William Sound,* a somber portrait of a dead eagle that eulogized the staggering losses and drove home the need for environmental protection against manmade disasters.

The 40 talented artists (including eight signature members of the Society of Animal Artists) represented in *Endangered Species: Flora & Fauna in Peril* build upon and extend this legacy, particularly in terms of biodiversity. Many of them have created works that form a careful, deeply felt record of species close to their homes or their hearts, such as Oscar Famili's portraits of the Key deer and Florida scrub jay, or Lotus McElfish's renditions of Texas snowbells and Texas wild-rice. Others have taken their inspiration from watershed events; for example, Shane Dimmick cites the release of gray wolves into Yellowstone National Park in 1995.

Still others have embraced a commitment to species in a particular region, like Arillyn Moran-Lawrence, who portrays the flora of Hawaii—the state with the greatest number of endangered plant species in the U.S. Some of the artworks extend beyond an individual species to depict an entire ecosystem, such as Peter Gaede's interpretation of California's Guadalupe-Nipomo Dunes Preserve and Katherine Beck's tribute to the endangered species of Kern County and Southern California.

The ability of art to heighten awareness of threatened and endangered species cannot be underestimated, a fact that is increasingly recognized at the local, state, and national levels. For example, Michael Riddet's tribute to the Sonora tiger salamander is part of an ongoing project called "Vanishing Circles," sponsored by the Priscilla V. and Michael C. Baldwin Foundation and donated to the Arizona-Sonora Desert Museum.

Perhaps most significant of all, art and artists help keep alive the hope for positive change despite the grave realities of species decimation. As scratchboard artist Diane Versteeg, who has worked as an animal keeper for over 30 years, states, "I hope my art shows my love and respect for animals and the natural world and encourages others to feel the same way toward the non-humans of this planet."

Endangered Species: Flora & Fauna in Peril was open to any living artist. Works were required to be original and not to have won any previous prize or award in another competition.

Eligible subject matter included any species officially listed as threatened or endangered by the U.S. Fish & Wildlife Service. A call for entries in the form of a prospectus was distributed by the Wildling Art Museum in the summer of 2006. To encourage entries, cash awards were offered for first, second, and third place.

Entries were evaluated in January 2008 by an eminently qualified, professional jury consisting of F. G. ("Eric") Hochberg, Ph.D., Curator of Invertebrate Zoology, Santa Barbara Museum of Natural History, Santa Barbara, CA; Hunter Hollins, Director, U.S. Department of the Interior Museum, Washington, D.C.; Amy Scott, Visual Art Curator, Autry Museum of the American West, Los Angeles, CA; and Karen Sinsheimer, Curator of Photography, Santa Barbara Museum of Art, Santa Barbara, CA.

Members of the jury were guided in their selections by clearly specified criteria. First priority was given to quality of artistry (composition and design, technique, etc.). The next priority encompassed factors relating to the diversity of the final selections for display, with special consideration given to species and habitats, geographic distribution, and media, styles, and techniques.

I hope this background information will add to your appreciation of the artworks depicted in this catalogue and the exhibition that it documents. I also hope that you will have the opportunity to view and enjoy *Endangered Species: Flora & Fauna in Peril* firsthand as it travels from Los Olivos, California, to Washington, D.C., and Parker, Colorado, in 2008-2009.

ESSAY

The Art of Saving Endangered Species

By Michael Tobias, Ph.D.

JANE GRAY MORRISON

Michael Tobias, Ph.D., *is president of the Dancing Star Foundation, a California-based non-governmental organization devoted to global biodiversity, conservation, animal protection, and environmental education (www.dancingstarfoundation.org). Author of over 35 books, and writer, director, and producer of over 100 films, Tobias has pursued field research in more than 75 countries. Most recently with his wife, Jane Gray Morrison (also a global ecologist, author, and film-maker), he authored* Sanctuary: Global Oases of Innocence *(Council Oak Books, 2008), which includes a foreword by Her Majesty The Queen of Bhutan. Tobias' and Morrison's latest PBS documentary is entitled* Hotspots, *a behind-the-scenes profile of what is truly working in conservation biology worldwide.*

THE PROMISE AND PERIL

The U.S. Fish & Wildlife Service (USFWS) is charged with proposing candidates for, and listing, threatened and endangered species under the authority of the 1973 Endangered Species Act (ESA). At the ESA's inception, 78 species appeared on the list. By the end of January 2008, the agency had designated 607 animal and 744 plant species. Four animal species currently have proposed status, while an additional 142 animal and 139 plant species are viewed as candidates for listing.

The goal, of course, is not merely to place species on a list. The USFWS has endeavored to provide a pragmatic, proactive mechanism for mitigating future threats to precious wildlife. Today, the agency has Habitat Conservation Plans in place for 730 species and Approved Recovery Plans for an additional 1,116 species.[1] Yet since 1973, only 22 species have recovered sufficiently to be removed from the list.[2]

The numbers represent far more than cold calculus. Each species has an amazing, mysterious face, an incalculable biography, and a primeval context that is local, regional, and global. These creatures harbor a common denominator: they are in dire jeopardy, usually as a result of actions by our own species. Over the millennia of our residence on Earth, our regard for creatures other than ourselves has vacillated. We have manifested actions and feelings ranging from the passion and enchantment of artists, scientists, and philosophers, to the unconditional love and reverence expressed by spiritual traditions and natural history enthusiasts, to far less flattering intentions and behaviors.

Given the extremes of the human animal, whose footprints are inordinately represented across the landscape, we

1. TESS, USFWS Threatened and Endangered Species System, http://ecos.fws.gov/tess_public/SummaryStatistics.do
2. TESS, http://ecos.fws.gov/tess_public/DelistingReport.do. See also J. Michael Scott, Dale D. Goble, and Frank W. Davis (eds.), *The Endangered Species Act at Thirty – Conserving Biodiversity in Human-Dominated Landscapes, Vol. 2* (Washington, D.C.: Island Press, 2006), 3.
3. E. O. Wilson, *The Creation – An Appeal to Save Life on Earth* (New York: W. W. Norton & Co., 2006), 74.
4. Joby Warrick, "Mass Extinction Underway, Majority of Biologists Say," *The Washington Post,* April 21, 1998, www.well.com/~davidu/extinction.html
5. 2006 Red List of Endangered Species, IUCN, www.iucn.org/themes/ssc/redlist2006/redlist2006.htm
6. The Associated Press, "California sees fewest butterflies in 40 years," May 10, 2006, http://msnbc.msn.com/id/12720318/print/1/displaymode/1098/
7. "The Road to Recovery," www.esasuccess.org/reports/
8. Op.cit., Wilson, 74.

must confront that all too familiar spectacle of ourselves: ungainly beasts in an innocent garden, with capacities that both recommend and condemn us in the context of biological history. Dire forces that we have helped unleash, like global warming and the "sixth spasm of extinctions" in the history of our planet, are solely our responsibility to rectify and mend.[3]

Art, the aesthetic conscience, the ability to celebrate and revere nature exemplified by this exhibition, is deeply woven throughout our evolution and today helps champion healing and mending even in the face of a shattering reality: at current trends, 40 to 60 percent of all life forms on Earth could vanish by the 22nd century, as reported by Joby Warrick of *The Washington Post* in 1998. Warrick wrote, "A majority of the nation's biologists are convinced that a 'mass extinction' of plants and animals is underway that poses a major threat to humans in the next century, yet most Americans are only dimly aware of the problem."[4]

Global data from the past 10 years validates the magnitude of this prediction. Worldwide, one third of all amphibians are now classified as threatened by the International Union for Conservation of Nature (IUCN). Among the so-called "evolutionarily distinct and globally endangered" amphibians, 85 percent "are receiving little or no conservation attention and will become extinct if action is not taken."[5] Since 2006, the IUCN has also identified 180 new creatures as being on the brink of extinction—putting the global total of all such species at 41,415. It must be noted that many species, such as the bryophytes (various groups of non-flowering plants), are scarcely considered in this estimate.

The effects are not remote, but rather can be observed close to home. As one example, in 2006 Californians witnessed a precipitous drop in the numbers of migrating butterflies. At one site, painted ladies *(Vanessa cardui)* declined from a recorded number of four per second to four per month.[6] Yet despite the devastation occurring in what has been, until quite recently, an unabashed Garden of Eden (as painted by Brueghel the Elder, Roelant Savery, Theodore Rousseau, John Martin, and countless others), it is imperative to focus on what works to restore that paradise.

The Quest to Save Lives

In 2006, the U.S. Senate declared May 11 as Endangered Species Day expressly to "encourage the people of the United States to become educated about, and aware of, threats to species, success stories in species recovery, and the opportunity to promote species conservation worldwide."[7] Among the 100 success stories reported in assessing the efficacy of the Endangered Species Act were the bald eagle, whooping crane, Kirtland's warbler, peregrine falcon, gray whale, Hawaiian goose, Virginia big-eared bat, and Big Bend gambusia.

Other species have not fared so well. For every success, there are many more declines, among them the North Atlantic right whale, the Indiana bat, eastern cougar (presumed extinct), red-cockaded woodpecker, Atlantic loggerhead sea turtle, puritan tiger beetle, seabeach amaranth, sandplain gerardia, American hart's tongue, and northeastern bulrush. Indeed, from 1973 (the year of the passage of the ESA) until the near present, over 100 species in the United States "have nevertheless vanished."[8]

Even without the human presence, all species go extinct eventually. What we see happening in our own lifetime, however, is astonishing. Of the 71 endemic Hawaiian bird taxa, 23

9. James D. Jacobi and Carter T. Atkinson, "Hawaii's Endemic Birds," in E.T. LaRoe, G. S. Farris, C. E. Puckett, P. D. Doran, & M. J. Mac (eds.), *Our living resources: a report to the nation on the distribution, abundance, and health of U.S. plants, animals, and ecosystems* (Washington, D.C.: U.S. Department of the Interior, National Biological Service, 1995), 376-381.

10. Richard Ellis, *No Turning Back – The Life and Death of Animal Species* (New York: HarperCollins, 2005), 153.

11. U.S. Fish & Wildlife Service, "Draft Revised Recovery Plan for the 'Alala (*Corvus hawaiiensis*)," December 2003, www.fws.gov/Endangered/federalregister/2003/03DEC.HTML

12. Michael Tobias, "Translocations in a Global Context," Dancing Star Foundation, DSF/Maungatautari Translocation Workshop, November 2006.

13. "Extremely Darwin: An Interview with Richard Dawkins," *California Wild* 51:1 (Winter 1998), www.calacademy.org/calwild/1998Winter/stories/Darwin.html. See also Craig Mortiz, "Conservation units and translocations: strategies for conserving evolutionary processes," *Hereditas* 130 (1999), 224.

14. www.esasuccess.org/reports/profile_pages/CaliforniaCondor.html

15. www.fws.gov/bisonrange/timeline.htm

are extinct and 30 are endangered or threatened.[9] In the case of the honeyeaters (*Meliphagidae* family) we have seen several go extinct, and one, the black face po'ouli (*Melamprosops phaeosoma*), is now considered the most endangered bird in the world with three known individuals remaining.[10]

The Hawaiian crow ('alala), an icon of indigenous spirituality, is in a similarly desperate situation. Endemic to the islands for several hundred thousand years, and still occupying its historical range as recently as 1890, the entire population now consists of a few dozen birds in captivity.[11] The last wild pair apparently disappeared in 2002, victims of introduced diseases and habitat loss—particularly koa wood extraction, nonnative fountain grass wildfires, domestic cattle grazing, and nonnative predators like mongooses, dogs, and feral cats. Such human-induced woes are certainly not unique to this species.[12]

Many techniques used by scientists, government authorities, and concerned citizens to save threatened and endangered species necessarily involve continued intervention and monitoring. This calls into question what we accomplish by our more intrusive endeavors. Some experts feel it would be better to let these endangered animals die out, sparing them the indignity of continued heavy human manipulation. Zoologist Richard Dawkins observes that natural selection has no foresight when it comes to human-induced events and suggests that our penchant for manipulation may have so-called "chosen benefits" that run counter to genetic benefits.[13]

On the other hand, careful manipulation has enabled us to resurrect creatures like the California condor (*Gymnogyps californianus*), American prairie bison (*Bison bison b.*), and brown pelican (*Pelecanus occidentalis*). All three species nearly went extinct. Condor numbers have gone from as few as 22

known birds to over 150;[14] bison, from as few as 325 in 1884 to nearly 300,000 today;[15] and eastern brown pelicans, for whom the first U.S. National Wildlife Refuge was created on Pelican Island, Florida, in 1903, from devastated numbers to 288,950 individuals just in North America.[16]

In Texas and Florida, authorities charged with saving the Florida panther opted to breed it with members of a subspecies, the Texas cougar, despite concerns of many taxonomists that this could set a dangerous precedent, the diffusion of a true species. Their numbers have surged from around 30 to well over 90 in the decade following the Texas/Florida endeavor.[17] Of special note, a set of strong incentive programs for private landowners, as outlined in the Multi-Species Recovery Plan for South Florida, have played a significant role in the panther's recovery.

THE TRUE COSTS OF CONSERVATION

Refreshingly, no financial profit has motivated the dramatic rejuvenations noted above; instead, they testify to the power of empathy and well-conceived conservation plans. The species' predicament spoke to some part of our own fragile experience, and our conscience replied. That is the essence of conservation biology, philanthropy, and art. With people doing the right thing—farmers caring for their land, ranchers respecting carrying capacity, volunteers rolling up their sleeves—much can happen at low cost.

Moreover, conservation is the best investment any society can make. Nature's services, which are free to all living creatures, have been translated into a minimum monetary value of several trillion dollars per year[18]—which puts expenditures to save species in a proper context. Take, for example, the ivory-billed woodpecker (*Campephilus principals*), presumed extinct

---

16. Some of the best data to gauge what happened to brown pelicans comes from recent studies by the Texas Parks and Wildlife Department, Endangered Resources Branch. They point out that between 1879 and 1918, the Texas brown pelican population went from 5,000 adults on just two islands to 5,000 birds in the entire state. By 1974, fewer than 10 breeding pairs remained in Texas. Similar decimations had taken place throughout the pelican's range. See www.tpwd.state.tx.us/publications/pwdpubs/media/pwd_bk_w7000_0013_eastern_brown_pelican.pdf. Audubon, who wrote of brown pelicans, "They are tough to kill," did not anticipate DDT. www.50states.com/bird/bpelican.htm. See also Allan Turner, "Brown pelican population soars," *Houston Chronicle*, February 8, 2008.

17. Joshua Dein, Kathryn Converse, and Christy Wolf, "Captive Propagation, Introduction, and Translocation Programs for Wildlife Vertebrates," *Journal of Zoo and Wildlife Medicine* 24, 265-270. See also Sylvia M. Fallon, "Genetic Data and the Listing of Species under the U.S. Endangered Species Act," *Conservation Biology* 21:5, 1186-1195. As Fallon points out, at least 38 decisions by the USFWS to list a species as endangered between February 1996 and February 2006 were predicated on genetic data.

18. Daphne Greenwood, "Natural Capitalism, Growth Theory and the Sustainability Debate," presented at the Southwest Economic Association meetings, Fort Worth, Texas, March 2001, http://web.uccs.edu/ccps/pdf/SWEA.2001v2..NATL%20CAP.pdf. Greenwood refers to a best estimate showing "gross world product of over $30 trillion (yielding) a stock value of over

for many decades. On April 28, 2005, scientists reported sighting a single bird in the Arkansas Cache River Wildlife Refuge. The USFWS responded quickly, committing $5.2 million for a population survey, $3.4 million for a habitat inventory, and $16 million more should the woodpecker's survival be confirmed.

This is serious money in the context of the U.S. budget for conservation. Of the 548 national wildlife refuges throughout America, at least 200 have no line items for staffing; and overall, the USFWS has an estimated $2.5 billion budget shortfall.[19] But in the context of the true value of nature, we cannot begin to ascertain the monetary value of a species. A salamander, a whale, a woodpecker—every one of these creatures is priceless.

Ultimately, it is habitat protection that can best ensure species protection. As of 2007, there were 114,007 protected areas on Earth encompassing approximately 4.7 billion acres, or 12 percent of the terrestrial planet.[20] That may not seem like much in global terms, but in just five of those acres, at Yasuni National Park in Ecuador, more than 700 tree species were discovered. Moreover, in the same park, Terry Erwin (a Smithsonian Institution entomologist) and his colleague Jonathan Coddington found so vast an assemblage of invertebrates as to extrapolate Amazonian insect and spider biodiversity per hectare (2.4 acres): an astonishing 60,000 species.[21]

This kind of data has pushed the number of estimated species on Earth to nearly 100 million.[22] The number may go higher following new biodiversity surveys of deep ocean and Antarctic habitats. Such data translates into an even more impressive and urgent imperative: act now, for there is so very much to lose.

THE ARTIST'S ROLE

In these circumstances, 21st century artists have opportunities like never before to make a difference in our relationship to and respect for life. Artists wake people up in ways that scientific data cannot. They reach into interpretive, subjective realms of emotion that transcend computational analysis. They reveal unprecedented perspectives, loyalty, and insight to help those who do not have the skills or interest to interpret the genetic nuances of a species like the Florida panther. Artists remind us that such creatures as the Sonora tiger salamander and white-flowering Hawaiian *Hibiscus arnottianus* are gorgeous, special beings, and we who share the world with them have the power to advocate for their beauty, their uniqueness, before we lose them altogether.

In less than a century, attitudes toward wildlife in the artistic and scientific communities have undergone a sea change. Audubon himself was often featured with a rifle in hand, as in the famed 1838 portrait by G. P. A. Healy. In his early years as a hunter, he did not flinch at the thought of shooting 100 birds in a day[23] and once declared that there was no way the passenger pigeon (*Ectopistes migratorius*) would ever be endangered, given what he rightly perceived to be the most numerous avian to grace the skies of North America.[24]

John Muir, who personally witnessed the horrific slaughter of the pigeons, was less confident when he wrote, "When the pigeon hunters attack the breeding-places they sometimes cut the timber from thousands of acres. Millions are caught in nets…(and) taken to New York, where they are sold for a cent apiece."[25] In 1914 Martha, the last known passenger pigeon, died at the Cincinnati Zoo. Audubon himself showed tremendous disappointment in later life at the excesses of his

$400 trillion" in 1997 dollars, though there is a robust debate over these figures—made more complicated by the fact no one can ethically assign a true value to standing forest or biodiversity, which are ultimately priceless. Paul Hawken, Amory Lovins, and Gretchen Dailey have been in the forefront of a lively discussion loosely characterized as "free nature's services." See Paul Hawken, "Natural Capitalism," *Mother Jones*, March/April 1997, www.motherjones.com/mother_jones/MA97/hawken.html

19. Josh Pollock, "Federal law works, but program is underfunded," *The Denver Post*, April 1, 2007, E1.
20. Michael Tobias and Jane Gray Morrison, *Sanctuary – Global Oases of Innocence* (San Francisco and Tulsa: Council Oak Books, 2008), xvii.
21. Bob Holmes and Gabrielle Walker, "How did paradise begin?" *New Scientist* 2048 (September 21, 1996), 34, www.newscientist.com/article/mg15120483.500
22. Terry Erwin, "The Tropical Forest Canopy: The Heart of Biotic Diversity," in E. O. Wilson (ed.), *Biodiversity* (Washington, D.C.: National Academy Press, 1988), 123-129; see also Terry Erwin, "Biodiversity at its Utmost: Tropical Forest Beetles" in M. L. Reaka-Kudla, D. E. Wilson, and E. O. Wilson (eds.), *Biodiversity II* (Washington, D.C.: Joseph Henry Press, 1997), 27-40.
23. Laura Harbold, "Drawn From Nature – Audubon's Artistic Legacy," www.neh.gov/news/humanities/2007-03/Audubon.htm

fellow humans as they continued to kill animals without the slightest hesitation.[26]

Today, wildlife artists prefer to observe without intrusion, and more and more scientists are finding nonlethal ways to study life. The days of building embalmed natural history collections are nearly over. Artists and scientists are finding new avenues to reach the public and advocate for change—a trend acknowledged and honored by the Wildling Art Museum and this exhibition.

THE CHALLENGE: IT'S NOT TOO LATE

For the millions of remaining species on this precious planet, it is still not too late. In the California Floristic Province, one of 35 global terrestrial hotspots (areas with the largest aggregates of native flowering plants), 73,451 km^2 out of a total of 293,804 km^2 remain undisturbed.[27] That is still a large amount of territory, and it does not begin to account for lands and waterways which can yet be restored.

Santa Barbara County, the home of the Wildling Art Museum, has at least 10 threatened and endangered species.[28] For just one of them, the Santa Barbara California tiger salamander (*Ambystoma californiense*), cost estimates for habitat protection range from $106 million to $418 million over the next 25 years.[29] Yet there are many ways for ordinary people to help this tiger salamander—among them, joining organizations like the Land Trust for Santa Barbara County, which has protected well over 13,000 acres to date.[30] Wherever we live, we can begin by nurturing and protecting the biological miracles of our neighborhoods—and by so doing, preserve the Earth itself for our children and grandchildren.

When Katharine Lee Bates wrote "America the Beautiful" in 1893 from a mountaintop in Colorado—and when Dr. Brewster Higley immortalized a place where "the buffalo roam, where the deer and the antelope play" in 1876 along the banks of Beaver Creek in Kansas—they were describing an era of greater innocence, unaware of the possibility that so many species could become extinct.

Today's artists are confronted with a chilling context in which to work, one that lends extraordinary importance to their poetic truths and sobering insights. The artists represented in *Endangered Species: Flora & Fauna in Peril* observe nature with exquisite care and attention, assuming their place in the long lineage of naturalist artists who have engaged with, rather than retreated from, the world. Never have the stakes been so intense, with so much life hanging in the balance, while we, as a species, choose how to act with our gifts, our power, and our conscience.

24. Errol Fuller, *Extinct Birds* (Oxford: Oxford University Press, 2000), 188.

25. Lisa Mighetto (ed.), *Muir Among the Animals – The Wildlife Writings of John Muir* (San Francisco: Sierra Club Books, 1986), 77.

26. Op.cit., Laura Harbold.

27. www.biodiversityhotspots.org/xp/Hotspots/california_floristic/

28. Los Padres National Forest, "Threatened and Endangered Species," www.redshift.com/~bigcreek/projects/natural_history/7th_meeting/Los%20Padres%20TES%20Species%20List.doc

29. U.S. Fish & Wildlife Service, "Costs of Conservation Actions for Santa Barbara County Population of California Tiger Salamander," October 7, 2004, www.fws.gov/news/NewsReleases/R1/79065134-C096-77DA-508F46B1D80FC3D8.html

30. www.sblandtrust.org

THE EXHIBITION

RACHELLE SIEGRIST

Crested Caracara, 2007

Opaque watercolor
on clayboard

Being a South Florida native, I have always loved crested caracaras. I have had the pleasure to interact with two caracaras up close at wildlife rehabilitation centers. It is unfortunate for this species that most injuries take place on highways or from gunshots. The bird in this painting was being treated and was due to be released after recovery.

WES SIEGRIST

Black-Footed Ferret, 2007

Opaque watercolor
on clayboard

The black-footed ferret's endangered status was precipitated indirectly through efforts to eradicate the black-tipped prairie dog. The ferret was considered extinct until 1981, when a rancher's dog brought home a dead one, leading to the discovery of a small colony in Wyoming. Their eventual reintroduction to the wild hinged on a sole male, "Scarface," who serves as a testament to the endangered species program.

JOY D. BARNES

Early Birds!, 2006

Digital photograph
with Ultrachrome inks
on Epson Premium
Luster paper

I hope to bring us back to a place where there is respect, understanding, and admiration for all living creatures and their environments. As part of this quest, I have journeyed to and photographed dune fields throughout the western United States. These tiny western snowy plovers were discovered during a hike in the Guadalupe-Nipomo Dunes Preserve in California. So vulnerable, yet so strong ... and so worth saving!

Photographed with permission of the Center for Natural Lands Management,
Rancho Guadalupe Dunes.

PETER GAEDE

A Naturalist's Encounter with Snowy Plovers, 2006

Watercolor/colored pencil on Arches watercolor paper

This painting was inspired by the sand dunes along the central California coast that include the Guadalupe-Nipomo Dunes Preserve. This complex ecosystem is home to a variety of uniquely adapted plants and animals. The western snowy plover breeds here and has been negatively impacted by habitat loss and off-road vehicle use. By looking at entire habitats, we can better understand and protect individual species living in them.

Concept and artwork by Peter Gaede; text in journal by Jennifer Rigby of Acorn Naturalists.

ANN HEFFERMAN

Oahu Tree Snails, 2007

Chalk pastel and
colored pencil on
Colourfix pastel paper

Oahu's high volcanic ridges are the native habitat of these tree snails. They exist nowhere else in the world, and from one ridge to the next, the species vary greatly. When their populations were thriving, they clustered on the backside of the leaves of trees such as the ohia lehua. In the breeze the shells made delicate, musical clinking sounds as they knocked against each other.

JOE WEATHERLY

Panthera onca, 2007

Oil on panel

A predator with power, strength, and speed, the jaguar is king of the tropical rain forests of Central and South America; it is also found in Arizona, New Mexico, and Texas. In this painting, the abstract design of the background is simplified to highlight the animal's form, pattern, and color, while simultaneously capturing an aura of mystery.

MICHAEL E. CALLES

The Lunch Counter, 2007

Oil on canvas

The grizzly bear represents all things wild to me. I have encountered bears numerous times over the years in the Yellowstone ecosystem and never fail to be amazed at their beauty and presence. I enjoy depicting large mammals because of their sculptural forms and the opportunity to elaborate on those forms with various paint qualities.

LINDA BESSE

The Return, 2007

Oil on gessoed board

I chose to paint whooping cranes because they characterize the important efforts we can use to help threatened and endangered wildlife. There are wonderful stories of recovery efforts for this species, from rehabilitating habitats to reestablishing migration routes with ultralights. The sight of a mating pair, calm and relaxed while feeding, is the most rewarding aspect of all.

D. L. ENGLE

Happy Bear, 2007

Bronze

The splendor of animals lies in experiencing the immediacy of their life force. In their presence I feel their energy, their power. They give themselves completely to every endeavor. Here, I witnessed the magic moment when a Louisiana black bear, in total bliss, abandoned all else to revel in falling water splashing on her back.

D. L. Engle

Puma Ways, 2007

Bronze

Being a cat involves, among other things, being never the least bit unaware. In less than an instant, a Florida panther can flash from tranquil leisure to brilliant focus. These opposites live astride the edge of a drawn sword in the big cats. The time that I spend with them is the most primal in feeling.

CHRIS CHAPMAN

California Jewelflower, 2007

Watercolor on Arches
watercolor paper

I wanted to paint the California jewelflower, whose beauty is legendary, but with no rain in the winter of 2007, I was unable to find a living specimen. So instead, I worked from photographs supplied by the Carrizo Plain Visitor Center and plants in the Santa Barbara Botanic Garden's herbarium collections. I felt honored to work from specimens collected by Ralph Hoffman in the 1930s and Dick Smith in the 1970s.

CHRIS CHAPMAN

Ventura Marsh Milk-Vetch, 2007

Watercolor on Arches
watercolor paper

The Ventura marsh milk-vetch had been presumed extinct, last seen in 1967, but in 1996 a biologist found it growing at a recently tarred construction site in Oxnard, California. Biologists from the University of California, Santa Barbara were then able to propagate seeds and grow them at Coal Oil Point. It is believed there are only 500 adult plants in the world.

JANET COLLINS

Canada Lynx Kitten, 2007

Digital photograph
on Fujicolor Crystal
Archive Lustre paper

During a wildlife trip in northern Montana, this innocent Canada lynx kitten stole my heart. It was the first time I had an opportunity to photograph a threatened species. None of my photos are computer enhanced, so I always take dozens of images in the field. I wish more people could experience seeing wildlife up close and realize how important it is to save their habitats.

SUZAN HAMILTON TODD

Falco #1, 2007
Falco #2, 2007

Mixed media, collage, recycled paper, wood, chalk, and paint

Born and raised in Brooklyn, New York, I learned at an early age to draw on my imagination and craft my own peace in a concrete jungle. My home is now in California's Santa Ynez Valley, and it is here that hawks and falcons first demonstrated themselves to me. I have become fascinated with birds of prey and drew these endangered northern aplomado falcons from photographs.

SHANE DIMMICK

Return, 2007

Acrylic on board

In 1995, a historic and controversial event occurred when 14 gray wolves were released in Yellowstone, 70 years after the species was exterminated in the park. In what is called a "trophic cascade," the elk are now stronger and the aspens and willows healthier with wolves present. As sure as Old Faithful, the return of the wolf has returned Yellowstone to a complete ecosystem.

SHANE DUERKSEN

Vanishing Point, 2007

Scratchboard

Champions of their terrain, bighorn sheep are truly remarkable when it comes to surviving on the cliffs. Their thick muscular bodies, sharp hooves, and balance allow them to traverse rocky slopes. Unable to adapt to different migratory routes, bighorns are on the decline. My objective for this piece was to create a visual flow using light and shadow. Scratchboard was the perfect medium to evoke this noble animal.

RAY BROWN

Plight of the Condor, 2007

Pencil on Bristol board

Working in pencil in black and white, I am somewhat of a rare bird myself. In depicting this California condor, I pushed the focal point high in the frame to create a dramatic image with the condor flying right overhead. Hopefully this piece will help keep the plight of the condor at the forefront as we pull this majestic bird back from its endangered status.

DEIAN MOORE

I Need Some Air, 2007

Oil on canvas

This painting is a statement not only about the green sea turtle that must rise for a breath of air, but also about the environmental conditions we face today. We don't just need air, we need clean air...we don't just need water, we need clean water. Without these two elements, both terrestrial and aquatic life will vanish.

KATHERINE R. BECK

Encroachment, 2007

Acrylic on canvas

In this painting, I chose to combine as many Kern County and Southern California endangered species as would reasonably fit, knowing that many species had to be excluded. I hope that Encroachment *conveys a message of what civilization threatens. I acknowledge that growth is required for an ever-expanding population, but that "smart growth" needs to be of the utmost concern to planning committees and voters alike.*

Arroyo toad, Bakersfield cactus, Blunt-nosed leopard lizard, California jewelflower, Giant garter snake, Kern primrose sphinx moth, Least Bell's vireo, Mohave tui chub, San Joaquin kit fox, and Tipton kangaroo rat.

DAVID C. GALLUP

Pacific Gold, 2005

Oil on birch ply

The western snowy plover is a familiar name in the conservation vs. development power struggle. The birds look the part—delicate, frail, and very beautiful—exactly like our coastal ecosystems. Being shy land-nesters, their numbers dwindle as we build on dunes and wetlands. Twenty years ago, I saw them every time I went to the beach. Now, it's a rare treat.

DAVID C. GALLUP

Fading Light on Carrington Point, 2006

Oil on jute (mounted)

You've probably never been to Carrington Point on California's Santa Rosa Island. With its rugged surf, jagged coast, and howling winds, it's not what most folks think of as paradise— unless they are artists, outdoor enthusiasts, or pelicans. Brown pelicans, nearly extinct when I was a boy, now flourish throughout their original habitat. To me, they represent the ability of our planet to heal itself.

NINA WARNER

Mountain Yellow-Legged Frog (Rana muscosa), 2007

Artist book with graphite and watercolor on gessoed paper

As an artist, I respond to nature and the experience of nature in my work. Through fishing and subsequent contact with field biologists, I learned that the mountain yellow-legged frog is disappearing primarily due to nonnative trout, habitat destruction, and pollution. I created a visual narrative of the frog using the book form: a reverse-fold binding with 10 pages of watercolor drawings.

AMY SADLE

Mesa Verde Cactus, 2007

Woodcut, monoprint, ink, and watercolor

Inspired by unconventional beauty, I enjoy interpreting cacti such as the endangered Mesa Verde cactus—a spine-wreathed cactus that bears translucent blooms. In this handmade, original print, I tried to illustrate the vulnerable size of the cactus in a vast, symbolic Mesa Verde landscape. I applied woodcut petroglyphs to an oil mono-print, finishing the piece with ink and watercolor.

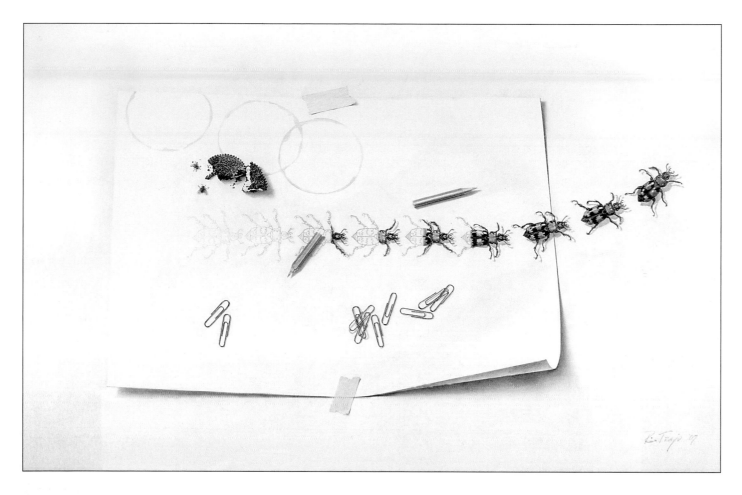

RAÚL TREJO

*American Burying
Beetle...Going, 2007*

Pencil and colored pencil
on Bristol board

*Insects have been the subjects of many of my art pieces. I am attracted to them in the aesthetic
sense, specifically beetles and butterflies. In the city, insects are mostly ignored or considered a
nuisance, and few people are concerned that some species are close to extinction, such as the
American burying beetle. I hope, at least in this piece of art, to immortalize this one.*

RICHARD LINDEKENS

Intensity, 2007

Digital photograph
on Fujicolor Crystal
Archive paper

In November each year, approximately 4,000 bald eagles gather along a six-mile stretch of the Chilkat River just north of Haines, Alaska. This particular section of the river provides some warm water upwelling. Because of this, numerous fish spawn late in the season and offer the eagles an opportunity to feed prior to the long winter.

RICHARD LINDEKENS

Safe Landing, 2007

Digital photograph
on Fujicolor Crystal
Archive paper

I had been taking photos of bald eagles for several hours around Homer, Alaska when this one presented itself. In the early 1970s, I worked in Alaska flying helicopters for the Bureau of Land Management. Being a pilot brought me very close to these birds. Over the years, thanks to some very concerned citizens and protection, they have made a great comeback.

PAT JACKMAN

Night Owl, 2007

Colored pencil on
Stonehenge paper

I was commissioned to draw this northern spotted owl from the Pacific Northwest region and became so engrossed that I stayed up all night in order to finish—hence the name Night Owl. *I tend to become obsessed by certain pieces in progress and can find it hard to lay my pencil down. For this piece, I used magnifying glasses similar to those worn by microsurgeons.*

PAT JACKMAN

Monkey See, 2007

Colored pencil on
illustration board

I seem to be drawn to the primates, as they are always entertaining. My inspiration for Monkey See *came on a very hot day while visiting the local zoo for reference photos. This particular red-backed squirrel monkey did not let the heat put him to sleep that day. I enjoy using black paper to portray longhaired animals, as I can detail individual hairs in this manner.*

OSCAR FAMILI

*Florida Scrub Jay in
the Northern Everglades
Watershed, 2007*

Oil on gessoboard

*The shy Florida scrub jay
is endangered in its
homeland, the northern
Everglades watershed.
Habitat loss from insecti-
cides, agricultural pollu-
tion, development, and managed water flow are pressuring this
elusive songbird. I sketched this one at a Zolfo Springs rescue
center. He was the only jay there. I painted him searching for a
mate in the unspoiled beauty of the Florida scrublands.*

OSCAR FAMILI

*Last Refuge of the Tiny
Key Deer (Big Pine Key,
Florida), 2007*

Oil on canvas

My family and I spent many sunny days at the National Key Deer Refuge on Big Pine Key, Florida. Over 600 tiny Key deer survive only here; the berries of the endangered silver thatch palm (far left) are a favorite food. The overarching black mangrove provides berries, leaves, and shelter. Two white ibis contrast with the diminutive size of the deer.

LOTUS MCELFISH

Texas Snowbells, 2007

Watercolor and graphite pencil on Arches water-color paper

After many calls to locate this specimen, I found that the San Antonio Botanical Gardens had a reclamation project. I also learned about David Bamberger, who searches out Texas snowbell colonies, collects seed, and reintroduces the plant. This portrait is in honor of his mission. The bloom is gorgeous and short-lived, dropping in masses that cover the ground like snow.

ARILLYN MORAN-LAWRENCE

Hibiscus arnottianus, 2007

Pen and ink on
museum board

I have visited Hawaii for decades, so I decided to become involved with Hawaiian plants. In 2007, I visited six botanical gardens and met with three botanists who introduced me to the endangered species. I studied, sketched, measured, painted, and photographed as many as possible. Hibiscus arnottianus has a gorgeous flower with large white petals set among deep green leaves.

LOTUS MCELFISH

Texas Wild-Rice, 2006

Watercolor on Arches
watercolor paper

Flo Oxley, botanist at the Ladybird Johnson Wildflower Center in Austin, suggested that I paint Texas wild-rice. This aquatic grass grows only in a small stretch of the upper San Marcos River. Its thin leaves, up to six feet long, wave in the currents among tubers and kayakers. At the San Marcos National Fish Hatchery, I sat beside a manmade stream to capture this flowing portrait.

JULIO J. PRO

Desert Monarch, 2006

Gouache on board

Bighorn sheep are very elusive and fascinating animals. I have seen them a few times in the wild, and the experience is memorable. There are so many textures in the coat and horns that reproducing them in paint becomes quite a challenge, which is why I picked this subject. In this piece, the animal is partially hidden in the shadows, which creates an interesting lighting situation.

MICHAEL JAMES RIDDET

Sonora Tiger Salamander,
2006

Acrylic on masonite

This salamander is part of a project called "Vanishing Circles," guided by a private foundation in collaboration with the Arizona-Sonora Desert Museum. It was chosen to illustrate one of the many threatened and endangered species found in the Sonoran Desert. I worked from reference photos of preserved salamanders courtesy of the museum.

PEGGY CROFT

Food for Thought, 2007

Pendant/brooch with sterling silver, 18K gold, 14K rose gold, hand-carved quartz crystal, and opals; display stand of sterling silver and malachite

An Alaskan cruise inspired Food For Thought. *Though we have successfully preserved the bald eagle, this piece shows how everything must be kept in balance. I feel strongly about keeping our waterways healthy, and the Chinook salmon feeds many wildlife species. In this pendant/brooch, I have integrated detailed figurative sculpting with layered carved crystal to create interesting optics.*

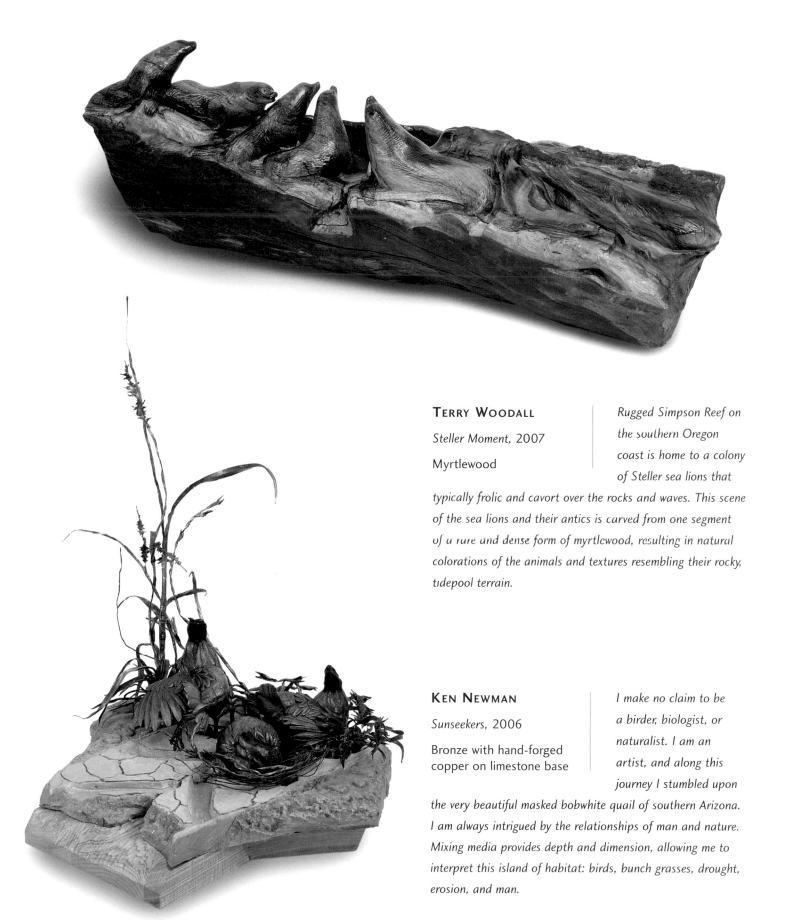

TERRY WOODALL

Steller Moment, 2007

Myrtlewood

Rugged Simpson Reef on the southern Oregon coast is home to a colony of Steller sea lions that typically frolic and cavort over the rocks and waves. This scene of the sea lions and their antics is carved from one segment of a rare and dense form of myrtlewood, resulting in natural colorations of the animals and textures resembling their rocky, tidepool terrain.

KEN NEWMAN

Sunseekers, 2006

Bronze with hand-forged copper on limestone base

I make no claim to be a birder, biologist, or naturalist. I am an artist, and along this journey I stumbled upon the very beautiful masked bobwhite quail of southern Arizona. I am always intrigued by the relationships of man and nature. Mixing media provides depth and dimension, allowing me to interpret this island of habitat: birds, bunch grasses, drought, erosion, and man.

KENT D. SAVAGE

Ocelot in Tree, 2006

Digital photograph
on Fujicolor Crystal
Archive paper

I photographed this ocelot at the Welder Wildlife Refuge in South Texas. As Texas has very few wildlife refuges, it is important to educate private landowners/ranchers about the value of preserving natural habitats. My interest is in promoting this awareness. At a ranch near my home, I have seen all the reclusive cats of South Texas—bobcats, cougars, jaguarundis, and ocelots.

MATHEW TEKULSKY

Willow Flycatcher, 2004

Digital photograph,
Lightjet Type C print

In May 2004, I was on the shores of Mono Lake in the eastern Sierra Nevada, watching the bird-banding activities of Point Reyes Bird Observatory biologists. When one of the biologists held a southwestern willow flycatcher in her hand, I had a chance to take a few photographs. This tiny bird has a powerful bite; it's hard to imagine any insect being able to break free.

JUNN ROCA

Evening Glow, 2007

Oil on linen

The silhouette of the old Santa Cruz cypress against the fading sunlight captured my imagination as I drove along the coast at Monterey, California. I rushed to do a quick color sketch to capture the serenity of the light. The muted colors of the sky serve as a background for the rugged texture of the rocks, while the towering trees stand witness to the eternal motion of the sea.

DEBBIE SULLIVAN

Vantage Point, 2007

Oil on canvas board

I was captivated and exhilarated by my first visit to Yellowstone National Park in September 2007. Unfortunately, I was unable to see the endangered gray wolf there. I was satisfied by a private game park, whose wolf pack gave me an insight into their social intricacies. The fall light illuminates the wolves and the edge on which they stand, a metaphor for their struggle to survive in the wild.

ANNE PEYTON

Balcones Black-Capped,
2007

Acrylic on watercolor
board

I love the challenge of trying to find a bird that is new to me. Two years ago, my goal was to observe a black-capped vireo, a small, beautiful bird found primarily in Texas. I finally located one at Balcones Canyonlands National Wildlife Refuge north of Austin. He was very secretive, singing while on top of the bushes, then quickly slipping under cover.

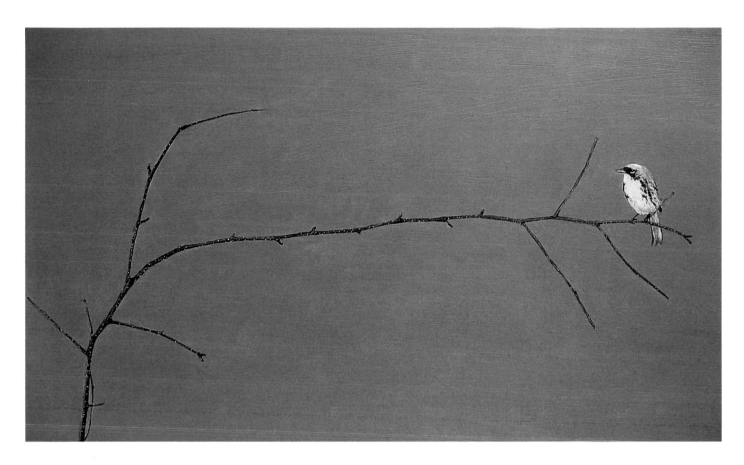

B.B. NELSON

The Kirtland's Warbler,
2007

Oil on panel

I grew up in Jamestown, New York, the birthplace of Roger Tory Peterson. His field guides have furthered the appreciation and study of birds for many people, including myself. The Kirtland's warbler nests in the forests of Michigan's Lower Peninsula and winters in the Bahamas. Its need for a very specific habitat has made it one of the rarest members of the warbler family.

DAN WOOD

Healthy Spirit, 2007

Digital photograph with
Epson pigment inks

This brown pelican sailed in the air curl of a six-foot wave near Pismo Beach, California. As the lead bird in a dramatic group formation, he flew high, stalled, and dove into the sea. After a fresh sardine dinner, he glided ashore and came to rest among 200 of his flock. This photo was taken after he dropped his head into a tapestry of feathers.

DAN WOOD

Salir del Huevo, 2007

Digital photograph with Epson pigment inks

A yellow crescent moon lit the waves landing on Tortuquero Beach, Costa Rica. The green sea turtle swam ashore with more than 50 possible babies inside her. Carefully, she made her way up the beach, and after leaving the eggs in a warm sand nest, she returned to the sea. Another mother swam ashore and disturbed the nest, breaking the egg seen here.

INES E. ROBERTS

Hawaiian Monk Seal, 2004

Digital photograph with Ultrachrome inks on Epson Ultra Premium Luster paper

This beautiful beach on Molokai was devoid of people and even birds. Then I saw the seal, snoozing in the sand near the breaking waves. He took no notice of me as I knelt at a safe distance. My guide from the nature preserve told me that it was a Hawaiian monk seal and that most people born on the island had never seen one. It was my lucky day.

DIANE VERSTEEG

Moose & Co., 2004

Scratchboard

"Moose" was a huge, handsome gray wolf that I knew well when I worked at Wolf Haven International. On this day a fly kept him company, and he alternated sniffing and snapping at it. I have worked as an animal keeper for over 30 years, and in my art, I try to portray each animal's personality, in addition to its strength, grace, and innocence.

DIANE VERSTEEG

Rosy II, 2004

Scratchboard

"Rosy" the grizzly bear lived with her brother at a zoo in Washington State. She never liked women and kept a close eye on all female keepers. I have loved and drawn animals since childhood. I hope my art shows my love and respect for animals and encourages others to feel the same way toward the non-humans of this planet.

EXHIBITION CHECKLIST

BARNES, JOY D. *(PAGE 18)*
Santa Barbara, California
Early Birds!, 2006
Digital photograph with Ultrachrome inks on Epson Premium Luster paper, 11.28 x 17 inches
> **Western snowy plover**
> *Charadrius alexandrinus nivosus*
> Status: Threatened
> Year Listed: 1993
> Where Listed: California, Oregon, Washington

BECK, KATHERINE R. *(PAGE 33)*
Bakersfield, California
Encroachment, 2007
Acrylic on canvas, 20 x 24 inches
> **Arroyo toad**
> *Bufo californicus*
> Status: Endangered
> Year Listed: 1994
> Where Listed: California

> **Bakersfield cactus**
> *Opuntia treleasei*
> Status: Endangered
> Year Listed: 1990
> Where Listed: California

> **Blunt-nosed leopard lizard**
> *Gambelia silus*
> Status: Endangered
> Year Listed: 1967
> Where Listed: California

> **California jewelflower**
> *Caulanthus californicus*
> Status: Endangered
> Year Listed: 1990
> Where Listed: California

> **Giant garter snake**
> *Thamnophis gigas*
> Status: Threatened
> Year Listed: 1993
> Where Listed: California

> **Kern primrose sphinx moth**
> *Euproserpinus euterpe*
> Status: Threatened
> Year Listed: 1980
> Where Listed: California

> **Least Bell's vireo**
> *Vireo bellii pusillus*
> Status: Endangered
> Year Listed: 1986
> Where Listed: California

> **Mohave tui chub**
> *Gila bicolor mohavensis*
> Status: Endangered
> Year Listed: 1970
> Where Listed: California

> **San Joaquin kit fox**
> *Vulpes macrotis mutica*
> Status: Endangered
> Year Listed: 1967
> Where Listed: California

> **Tipton kangaroo rat**
> *Dipodomys nitratoides nitratoides*
> Status: Endangered
> Year Listed: 1988
> Where Listed: California

BESSE, LINDA *(PAGE 23)*
Mead, Washington
The Return, 2007
Oil on gessoed board, 14.75 x 24 inches
> **Whooping crane**
> *Grus americana*
> Status: Endangered
> Year listed: 1967
> Where Listed: Colorado, Kansas, Montana, Nebraska, North Dakota, Oklahoma, South Dakota, Texas

BROWN, RAY *(PAGE 31)*
Lake Forest, California
Plight of the Condor, 2007
Pencil on Bristol board, 12 x 16 inches
> **California condor**
> *Gymnogyps californianus*
> Status: Endangered
> Year Listed: 1967
> Where Listed: California, Arizona, Utah

CALLES, MICHAEL E. *(PAGE 22)*
Brigham, Utah
The Lunch Counter, 2007
Oil on canvas, 16 x 20 inches
> **Grizzly bear**
> *Ursus arctos horribilis*
> Status: Threatened
> Year Listed: 1967
> Where Listed: Idaho, Montana, Washington, Wyoming

CHAPMAN, CHRIS *(PAGE 26)*
Goleta, California
California Jewelflower, 2007
Watercolor on Arches watercolor paper, 15 x 8 inches
> **California jewelflower**
> *Caulanthus californicus*
> Status: Endangered
> Year Listed: 1990
> Where Listed: California

CHAPMAN, CHRIS *(PAGE 26)*
Goleta, California
Ventura Marsh Milk-Vetch, 2007
Watercolor on Arches watercolor paper,
10.5 x 7 inches

> **Ventura marsh milk-vetch**
> *Astragalus pycnostachyus* var.
> *lanosissimus*
> Status: Endangered
> Year Listed: 2001
> Where Listed: California

COLLINS, JANET *(PAGE 27)*
Sedona, Arizona
Canada Lynx Kitten, 2007
Digital photograph on Fujicolor Crystal
Archive Lustre paper, 10 x 14 inches

> **Canada lynx**
> *Lynx canadensis*
> Status: Threatened
> Year Listed: 2000
> Where Listed: Colorado, Idaho,
> Maine, Michigan, Minnesota,
> Montana, New Hampshire,
> New York, Oregon, Utah,
> Vermont, Washington,
> Wisconsin, Wyoming

CROFT, PEGGY *(PAGE 48)*
Los Angeles, California
Food for Thought, 2007
Pendant/brooch with sterling silver,
18K gold, 14K rose gold, hand-carved
quartz crystal, and opals; display stand
of sterling silver and malachite
2.5 x 2.5 x 4.5 inches

> **Bald eagle**
> *Haliaeetus leucocephalus*
> Status: Formerly endangered;
> delisted in 2007 (lower 48 states
> and District of Columbia)
> Year Listed: 1967
> Where Listed: Relisted in 2008
> in the Sonoran Desert region of
> central Arizona

Chinook salmon
Oncorhynchus tshawytscha
Status: Endangered
Year Listed: 1999
Where Listed: Idaho, Oregon,
Washington, California

DIMMICK, SHANE *(PAGE 29)*
Westcliffe, Colorado
Return, 2007
Acrylic on board, 20 x 17 inches

> **Gray wolf**
> *Canis lupus*
> Status: Endangered
> Year Listed: 1967
> Where Listed: Arizona,
> Colorado, Idaho, Illinois,
> Indiana, Iowa, Missouri,
> Montana, New Mexico,
> North Dakota, Ohio,
> South Dakota, Washington,
> Wyoming

DUERKSEN, SHANE *(PAGE 30)*
Denver, Colorado
Vanishing Point, 2007
Scratchboard, 11 x 18 inches

> **Bighorn sheep**
> *Ovis canadensis*
> Status: Endangered
> Year Listed: 1998
> Where Listed: California

ENGLE, D. L. *(PAGE 24)*
Valinda, California
Happy Bear, 2007
Bronze, 5 x 4 x 3.75 inches

> **Louisiana black bear**
> *Ursus americanus luteolus*
> Status: Threatened
> Year Listed: 1992
> Where Listed: Louisiana,
> Mississippi, Texas

ENGLE, D. L. *(PAGE 25)*
Valinda, California
Puma Ways, 2007
Bronze, 16 x 14.25 x 8 inches

> **Florida panther**
> *Puma concolor coryi*
> Status: Endangered
> Year Listed: 1967
> Where Listed: Florida

FAMILI, OSCAR *(PAGE 42)*
North Miami Beach, Florida
*Florida Scrub Jay in the Northern
Everglades Watershed,* 2007
Oil on gessoboard, 24 x 12 inches

> **Florida scrub jay**
> *Aphelocoma coerulescens*
> Status: Threatened
> Year Listed: 1987
> Where Listed: Florida

FAMILI, OSCAR *(PAGE 43)*
North Miami Beach, Florida
*Last Refuge of the Tiny Key Deer
(Big Pine Key, Florida),* 2007
Oil on canvas, 14 x 28 inches

> **Key deer**
> *Odocoileus virginianus clavium*
> Status: Endangered
> Year Listed: 1967
> Where Listed: Florida

GAEDE, PETER *(PAGE 19)*
Santa Barbara, California
*A Naturalist's Encounter with
Snowy Plovers,* 2006
Watercolor/colored pencil on Arches
watercolor paper, 16 x 24 inches

> **Western snowy plover**
> *Charadrius alexandrinus nivosus*
> Status: Threatened
> Year Listed: 1993
> Where Listed: California,
> Oregon, Washington

GALLUP, DAVID C. *(PAGE 35)*
Thousand Oaks, California
Fading Light on Carrington Point, 2006
Oil on jute (mounted), 12 x 12 inches
> **Brown pelican**
> *Pelecanus occidentalis*
> Status: Endangered
> Year Listed: 1970
> Where Listed: California,
> Louisiana, Mississippi, Oregon,
> Puerto Rico, Texas, Virgin Islands,
> Washington

GALLUP, DAVID C. *(PAGE 34)*
Thousand Oaks, California
Pacific Gold, 2005
Oil on birch ply, 18 x 18 inches
> **Western snowy plover**
> *Charadrius alexandrinus nivosus*
> Status: Threatened
> Year Listed: 1993
> Where Listed: California,
> Oregon, Washington

HEFFERMAN, ANN *(PAGE 20)*
Santa Barbara, California
Oahu Tree Snails, 2007
Chalk pastel and colored pencil
on Colourfix pastel paper,
14 x 10.5 inches
> **Oahu tree snail**
> *Achatinella decipiens*
> Status: Endangered
> Year Listed: 1981
> Where Listed: Hawaii

JACKMAN, PAT *(PAGE 41)*
Salem, Oregon
Monkey See, 2007
Colored pencil on illustration board,
9 x 15 inches
> **Red-backed squirrel monkey**
> *Saimiri oerstedii*
> Status: Endangered
> Year Listed: 1970
> Where Listed: Costa Rica, Panama

JACKMAN, PAT *(PAGE 40)*
Salem, Oregon
Night Owl, 2007
Colored pencil on Stonehenge paper,
14 x 11 inches
> **Northern spotted owl**
> *Strix occidentalis caurina*
> Status: Threatened
> Year Listed: 1990
> Where Listed: California,
> Oregon, Washington

LINDEKENS, RICHARD *(PAGES 38-39)*
Santa Ynez, California
Intensity, 2007
Digital photograph on Fujicolor Crystal
Archive paper, 9.5 x 12.5 inches

Safe Landing, 2007
Digital photograph on Fujicolor Crystal
Archive paper, 11.25 x 17.25 inches
> **Bald eagle**
> *Haliaeetus leucocephalus*
> Status: Formerly endangered;
> delisted in 2007 (lower 48 states
> and District of Columbia)
> Year Listed: 1967
> Where Listed: Relisted in 2008
> in the Sonoran Desert region of
> central Arizona

McELFISH, LOTUS *(PAGE 44)*
Spring Branch, Texas
Texas Snowbells, 2007
Watercolor and graphite pencil
on Arches watercolor paper,
20.25 x 16.75 inches
> **Texas snowbells**
> *Styrax platanifolius texanus*
> Status: Endangered
> Year Listed: 1984
> Where Listed: Texas

McELFISH, LOTUS *(PAGE 45)*
Spring Branch, Texas
Texas Wild-Rice, 2006
Watercolor on Arches watercolor paper,
18 x 27 inches
> **Texas wild-rice**
> *Zizania texana*
> Status: Endangered
> Year Listed: 1978
> Where Listed: Texas

MOORE, DEIAN *(PAGE 32)*
Blodgett, Oregon
I Need Some Air, 2007
Oil on canvas, 24 x 12 inches
> **Green sea turtle**
> *Chelonia mydas*
> Status: Endangered/Threatened
> Year Listed: 1978
> Where Listed: Endangered
> in Florida and Mexico;
> Threatened in Alabama, California,
> Connecticut, Delaware, Georgia,
> Hawaii, Louisiana, Maryland,
> Mississippi, New York, North
> Carolina, Oregon, Puerto Rico,
> South Carolina, Texas, Virgin
> Islands, Virginia, Washington

MORAN-LAWRENCE, ARILLYN *(PAGE 45)*
San Juan Capistrano, California
Hibiscus arnottianus, 2007
Pen and ink on museum board,
13.5 x 17 inches
> **White hibiscus (Koki`o ke`oke`o)**
> *Hibiscus arnottianus immaculatus*
> Status: Endangered
> Year listed: 1992
> Where Listed: Hawaii

NELSON, B. B. *(PAGE 55)*
Gray, Maine
The Kirtland's Warbler, 2007
Oil on panel, 12 x 24 inches
> **Kirtland's warbler**
> *Dendroica kirtlandii*
> Status: Endangered
> Year Listed: 1967
> Where Listed: Michigan,
> South Carolina, Wisconsin

NEWMAN, KEN *(PAGE 49)*
Cambridge, Idaho
Sunseekers, 2006
Bronze with hand-forged copper on
limestone base, 30 x 21 x 21 inches
> **Masked bobwhite quail**
> *Colinus virginianus ridgwayi*
> Status: Endangered
> Year Listed: 1967
> Where Listed: Arizona

PEYTON, ANNE *(PAGE 54)*
Phoenix, Arizona
Balcones Black-Capped, 2007
Acrylic on watercolor board,
11 x 14 inches
> **Black-capped vireo**
> *Vireo atricapilla*
> Status: Endangered
> Year Listed: 1987
> Where Listed: Kansas,
> Louisiana, Oklahoma, Texas

PRO, JULIO J. *(PAGE 46)*
Northridge, California
Desert Monarch, 2006
Gouache on board, 17 x 14 inches
> **Bighorn sheep**
> *Ovis canadensis*
> Status: Endangered
> Year Listed: 1998
> Where Listed: California

RIDDET, MICHAEL JAMES *(PAGE 47)*
Gays Mills, Wisconsin
Sonora Tiger Salamander, 2006
Acrylic on masonite, 16 x 12 inches
> **Sonora tiger salamander**
> *Ambystoma tigrinum stebbinsi*
> Status: Endangered
> Year Listed: 1997
> Where Listed: Arizona

ROBERTS, INES E. *(PAGE 57)*
Santa Barbara, California
Hawaiian Monk Seal, 2004
Digital photograph with Ultrachrome
inks on Epson Ultra Premium Luster
paper, 12 x 18 inches
> **Hawaiian monk seal**
> *Monachus schauinslandi*
> Status: Endangered
> Year Listed: 1976
> Where Listed: Hawaii

ROCA, JUNN *(PAGE 52)*
Sunland, California
Evening Glow, 2007
Oil on linen, 17 x 12 inches
> **Santa Cruz cypress**
> *Cupressus abramsiana*
> Status: Endangered
> Year Listed: 1987
> Where Listed: California

SADLE, AMY *(PAGE 36)*
Syracuse, Nebraska
Mesa Verde Cactus, 2007
Woodcut, monoprint, ink, and
watercolor, 26 x 20 inches
> **Mesa Verde cactus**
> *Sclerocactus mesae-verdae*
> Status: Threatened
> Year Listed: 1979
> Where Listed: Colorado,
> New Mexico

SAVAGE, KENT D. *(PAGE 50)*
Sandia, Texas
Ocelot in Tree, 2006
Digital photograph on Fujicolor
Crystal Archive paper, 16 x 20 inches
> **Ocelot**
> *Leopardus pardalis*
> Status: Endangered
> Year Listed: 1972
> Where Listed: Arizona, Texas

SIEGRIST, RACHELLE *(PAGE 16)*
Townsend, Tennessee
Crested Caracara, 2007
Opaque watercolor on clayboard,
3.5 x 3.5 inches
> **Audubon's crested caracara**
> *Polyborus plancus audubonii*
> Status: Threatened
> Year Listed: 1987
> Where Listed: Florida

SIEGRIST, WES *(PAGE 17)*
Townsend, Tennessee
Black-Footed Ferret, 2007
Opaque watercolor on clayboard,
4.5 x 3.5 inches
> **Black-footed ferret**
> *Mustela nigripes*
> Status: Endangered
> Year Listed: 2000
> Where Listed: Arizona,
> Colorado, Montana,
> South Dakota, Utah, Wyoming

SULLIVAN, DEBBIE *(PAGE 53)*
Esperance, Western Australia
Vantage Point, 2007
Oil on canvas board, 15 x 24 inches
> **Gray wolf**
> *Canis lupus*
> Status: Endangered
> Year Listed: 1967
> Where Listed: Arizona, Colorado,
> Idaho, Illinois, Indiana, Iowa,
> Missouri, Montana, New Mexico,
> North Dakota, Ohio, South
> Dakota, Washington, Wyoming

TEKULSKY, MATHEW *(PAGE 51)*
Los Angeles, California
Willow Flycatcher, 2004
Digital photograph, Lightjet Type C
print, 20 x 30 inches
> **Southwestern willow flycatcher**
> *Empidonax traillii extimus*
> Status: Endangered
> Year Listed: 1995
> Where Listed: Arizona, California,
> Colorado, Nevada, New Mexico,
> Texas, Utah

TODD, SUZAN HAMILTON *(PAGE 28)*
Buellton, California
Falco #1, 2007
Falco #2, 2007
Mixed media, collage, recycled
paper, wood, chalk, and paint;
18 x 30 inches each
> **Northern aplomado falcon**
> *Falco femoralis septentrionalis*
> Status: Endangered
> Year Listed: 1986
> Where Listed: Texas

TREJO, RAÚL *(PAGE 37)*
San Ysidro, California
American Burying Beetle...Going, 2007
Pencil and colored pencil on Bristol
board, 16 x 24.5 inches
> **American burying beetle**
> *Nicrophorus americanus*
> Status: Endangered
> Year Listed: 1989
> Where Listed: Arkansas,
> Massachusetts, Michigan,
> Nebraska, Ohio, Oklahoma,
> Rhode Island, South Dakota

VERSTEEG, DIANE *(PAGE 58)*
Spokane Valley, Washington
Moose & Co., 2004
Scratchboard, 9.5 x 15 inches
> **Gray wolf**
> *Canis lupus*
> Status: Endangered
> Year Listed: 1967
> Where Listed: Arizona, Colorado,
> Idaho, Illinois, Indiana, Iowa,
> Missouri, Montana, New Mexico,
> North Dakota, Ohio, South
> Dakota, Washington, Wyoming

VERSTEEG, DIANE *(PAGE 59)*
Spokane Valley, Washington
Rosy II, 2004
Scratchboard, 10 x 13 inches
> **Grizzly bear**
> *Ursus arctos horribilis*
> Status: Threatened
> Year Listed: 1967
> Where Listed: Idaho, Montana,
> Washington, Wyoming

WARNER, NINA *(PAGE 36)*
Santa Barbara, California
Mountain Yellow-Legged Frog
(Rana muscosa), 2007
Artist book with graphite and
watercolor on gessoed paper,
5.5 x 7.5 inches, opens to 20 inches
> **Mountain yellow-legged frog**
> *Rana muscosa*
> Status: Endangered
> Year Listed: 2002
> Where Listed: California, Nevada

WEATHERLY, JOE *(PAGE 21)*
Santa Ana, California
Panthera onca, 2007
Oil on panel, 12 x 24 inches
> **Jaguar**
> *Panthera onca*
> Status: Endangered
> Year Listed: 1972
> Where Listed: Arizona,
> New Mexico, Texas

WOOD, DAN *(PAGE 56)*
Santa Cruz, California
Healthy Spirit, 2007
Digital photograph with Epson
pigment inks, 13 x 19 inches
> **Brown pelican**
> *Pelecanus occidentalis*
> Status: Endangered
> Year Listed: 1970
> Where Listed: California,
> Louisiana, Mississippi,
> Oregon, Puerto Rico, Texas,
> Virgin Islands, Washington

WOOD, DAN *(PAGE 57)*
Santa Cruz, California
Salir del Huevo, 2007
Digital photograph with Epson
pigment inks, 19 x 13 inches
> **Green sea turtle**
> *Chelonia mydas*
> Status: Endangered/Threatened
> Year Listed: 1978
> Where Listed: Endangered
> in Florida and Mexico;
> Threatened in Alabama, California,
> Connecticut, Delaware, Georgia,
> Hawaii, Louisiana, Maryland,
> Mississippi, New York, North
> Carolina, Oregon, Puerto Rico,
> South Carolina, Texas, Virgin
> Islands, Virginia, Washington

WOODALL, TERRY *(PAGE 49)*
North Bend, Oregon
Steller Moment, 2007
Myrtlewood, 11 x 30 x 9 inches
> **Steller sea lion**
> *Eumetopias jubatus*
> Status: Threatened
> Year Listed: 1990
> Where Listed: Alaska,
> California, Oregon,
> Washington